POISON IN ANIMALS

PHILIP STREET

Poison in Animals

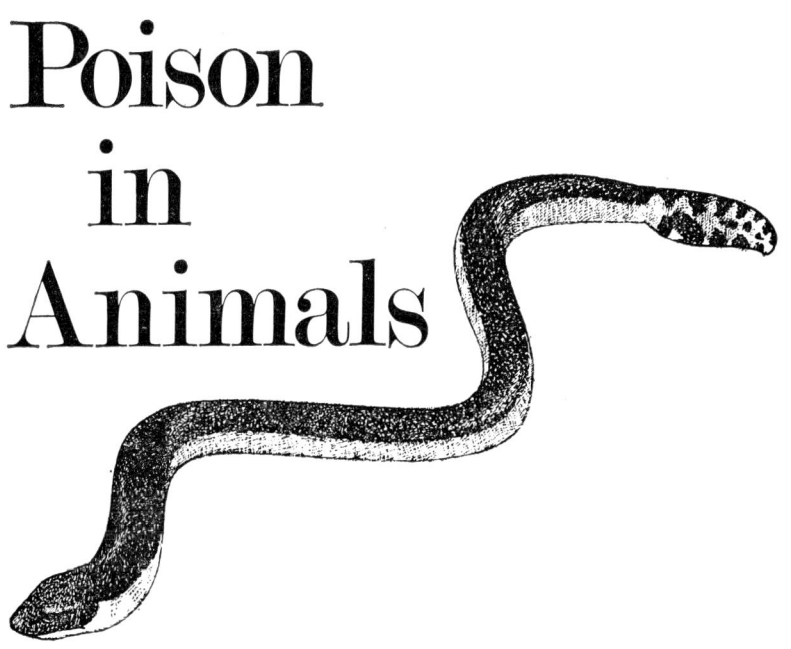

Illustrated by Carol Lawson

KESTREL BOOKS

KESTREL BOOKS
Published by Penguin Books Ltd
Harmondsworth, Middlesex, England

Copyright © 1978 by Philip Street
Illustrations Copyright © 1978 by Carol Lawson

All rights reserved. No part of this publication may be
reproduced, stored in a retrieval system, or transmitted in any
form or by any means, electronic, mechanical, photocopying,
recording, or otherwise, without the prior permission of the
Copyright owner.

First published 1978

ISBN 0 7226 5423 5

Printed in Great Britain by
Richard Clay (The Chaucer Press) Ltd,
Bungay, Suffolk

Contents

	Introduction	7
1	The Venomous Bite	9
2	The Venomous Snakes	24
3	Poison Spines and Hairs	39
4	Microscopic Sting Cells	54
5	Poisoning by Sting	63
6	Chemical Warfare	76
	Index	96

Introduction

Throughout history poison has been the chosen weapon of many an assassin, and death by poisoning is a favourite theme for the thriller writer. Poisons, and poisoning, are endlessly fascinating subjects.

But man is not alone in using poison to kill. One of the most interesting aspects of natural history is the variety of methods used by animals to poison one another. Have you ever watched a fly land on and be ensnared in a spider's web? Immediately the spider rushes out from its hidden lair, alerted by the vibrations of the struggling fly. Almost as soon as the spider reaches its victim the struggles cease. The spider's hollow fangs have gripped the fly and sunk into its flesh, at the same instant pumping in one of the most virulent poisons known, killing the fly almost instantly.

Most animal poisons are used against other animals, but many of them are also capable of killing humans. The worst of these are the ones produced by venomous snakes, and tens of thousands of people in various parts of the world are killed every year by snake bite. But snakes are not the only animals capable of killing man with their venom. If you live on the east coast of Australia you will be well aware of the danger of being attacked and killed by sharks if you venture into the water for a swim. But there is an even greater danger, which you are not likely to see as you are swimming. This is a tiny jellyfish with a harmless sounding name. It is called the sea wasp, an almost invisible creature not many centimetres across, but so powerfully armed with deadly sting cells that you may well be dead within minutes if you bump into it.

This book is about the great variety of ways in which animals are able to poison one another, sometimes in defence and sometimes in attack. It may help you to recognize and avoid a dangerous situation if you are unlucky enough to find yourself on the brink of one. But this is not the main purpose of the book – fortunately relatively few people are likely to be confronted by a shark, let alone a sea wasp. What the book does try to show is the fascination, and sometimes even beauty, of one aspect of animal behaviour.

1
The Venomous Bite

Teeth are among the more important weapons which animals use both in attack and defence. Some animals do more than bite when they use their teeth or jaws – at the same time they actually inject poison from their saliva into the wound. The poisonous bite is best known and most widespread among the spiders and the venomous snakes, but there are other animals which use it too.

Shrews and moles

Shrews are among the smallest, the most ferocious and the most aggressive of all mammals. An equally ferocious large mammal would be quite terrifying. They cannot even tolerate members of their own species. If two shrews should meet, unless they happen to be a male and a female at the breeding season, a fierce fight ensues. They are also extremely hungry little creatures. They must eat their own weight of food every day, and cannot go without food for more than a few hours. As a result they will attack, kill and eat any small animal they can overpower.

Two shrews fighting. If no other food is available, they will eat each other. Usually, though, they eat insects.

The most interesting thing about shrews, however, is that, so far as we know, they are the only mammals to have a venomous bite. For hundreds of years it was said that the bite of the shrew was poisonous. Then came the modern scientist, who dismissed the idea as nothing more than an example of ignorant superstition. The first to doubt this modern scientific wisdom was an American zoologist, C. J. Maynard. In 1889 he was bitten on the hand by one of the larger American shrews, *Blarina brevicauda*. To his amazement, although the shrew's teeth had only just punctured his skin, he felt an immediate burning sensation, which was fol-

THE VENOMOUS BITE

lowed by shooting pains all up his arm. These largely subsided after about an hour, but some discomfort lasted for more than a week.

No one, however, took any notice of his findings, and it was not until 1942 that another American, O. P. Pearson, also became interested in the age-old stories of the poisonous bite of the shrew, and decided to make a thorough investigation. He made extracts of the salivary glands of the shrew and then injected measured quantities into mice. Now the shrew has two pairs of salivary glands. One pair, the parotid glands, are in the shrew's cheeks; the other pair, the submaxillary glands, lie beneath the tongue in the lower jaw. Pearson discovered that extracts of the parotid glands injected into the veins of mice had no adverse effects no matter how much was injected. But with the submaxillary glands the story was very different. A small quantity equivalent to no more than sixty millionths of their body weight killed all the mice in less than six minutes and an equivalent dose killed rabbits in about the same time.

So far no other mammal has been proved to possess a toxic saliva, but further research may well show that the mole is similarly endowed. Moles are quite closely related to shrews, and have a similar need to consume large quantities of food every day. They prey mainly upon earthworms, and it is known that they are able to paralyse them by biting them near the front end. These living but paralysed worms can then be stored indefinitely in the mole's fortress until they are needed. (Dead worms would of course soon begin to decay.) It would not be surprising to find that the paralysing bite is achieved through a toxic saliva.

A mole paralysing an earthworm by biting it. As the picture shows, moles have powerful front claws which allow them to dig rapidly through soil in search of worms.

Moray eel

Many fish have formidable teeth, as for example the sharks, the piranhas and the barracudas, but only one kind of fish, so far as we know, has a poisonous bite. This is the moray eel, a fairly large eel about one metre long and armed with an array of needle-sharp teeth. These would be bad enough in themselves, but they are made much worse because the saliva which they

THE VENOMOUS BITE

carry into the wound is poisonous. Moray eels are a menace to skin divers and spear fishermen, for they live in old wrecks, rock crevices and underwater caves. They are extremely aggressive creatures, and will swim out to attack any unsuspecting diver who approaches their lair.

A moray eel ready to attack a diver with its savage bite.

Ringed octopus

With its eight long arms or tentacles lined with very effective suckers, its bag-like body and its intelligent-looking eyes, the octopus doesn't look in the least like a snail. Yet it is indeed a mollusc: it has a mouth which is hidden by the ring of arms. Its horny jaws are shaped very much like the beak of a parrot, and they are capable of giving a painful and serious bite. Octopuses generally are quite docile and remarkably intelligent creatures. They are not very large, the common octopus having a body about the size of a football, and a maximum arm span of about two and a half metres.

There is, however, one extremely dangerous species, the ringed octopus. Curiously, it is one of the smallest, with a body not more than a few centimetres across. It is also one of the most beautiful. The background colour is yellowish, with decorations of vivid bluish purple markings all over the body and the arms. If the animal is disturbed these markings become even more intense. Ringed octopuses belong to Australia, where they live in shore rock pools and in shallow offshore waters.

The fact that they are dangerously venomous was not discovered until the 1950s. Most people have a healthy respect for octopuses, and prefer to look at them rather than touch them or pick them up. One keen naturalist, however, was so fascinated when he discovered one of these tiny octopuses in a rock pool near Sydney that he picked it up and placed it on his

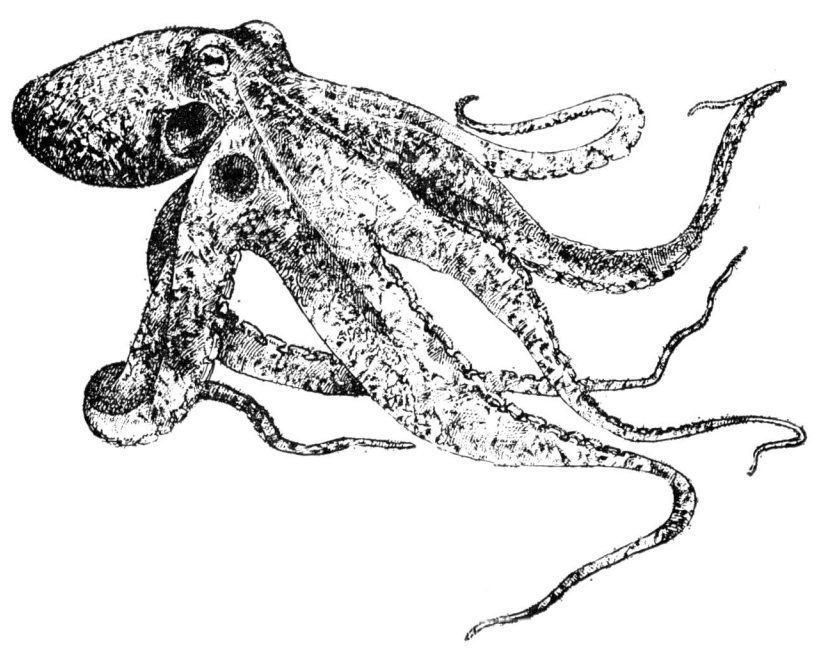

The ringed octopus is very dangerous because it combines excellent eyesight with an extremely venomous bite. Like all octopuses, its eyes are high up on its body which means it can see most things approaching.

arm in order to look at it more closely. But the octopus did not appreciate his attentions, and bit him. He began to feel the effects of the bite almost immediately, and despite all efforts to retrieve him, he died an hour and a half later. Not long after this another naturalist captured a ringed octopus and slung it over his shoulder to carry it up the beach. It bit his neck, and within two hours he, too, was dead. So far no cure or antidote for the bite of the ringed octopus has been discovered.

Snails

A snail eats by means of a remarkable structure known as the radula, which in most species consists of a long ribbon of tissue set with hundreds, even thousands, of microscopic teeth arranged in a number of parallel rows. The radula itself is mounted on a movable proboscis. Normally the proboscis remains inside the mouth, but when the snail is feeding it is protruded through the mouth and the radula is scraped backwards and forwards over the surface of the food, which

A diagram of a snail showing how the radula is kept inside its mouth, like a tongue, until needed to scrape some food. The snail's eyes are situated at the top of a pair of long tentacles which act like periscopes.

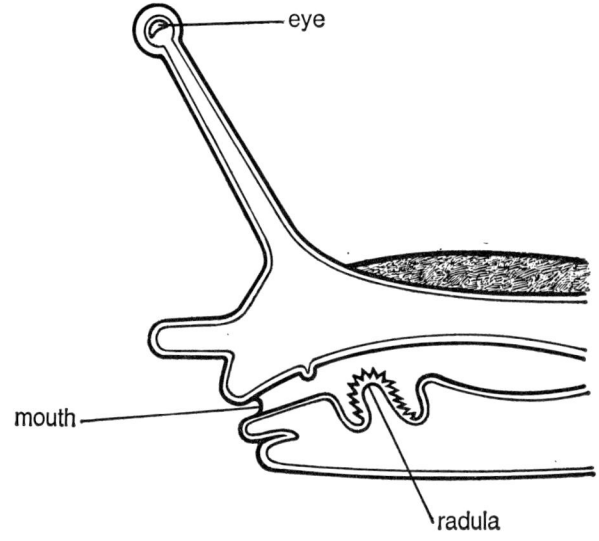

THE VENOMOUS BITE

may be plant or animal. It acts like a file, scraping off minute particles of food which are passed back into the mouth to be swallowed. The radula grows continuously through the life of the snail, so that as the teeth on one part wear out, the next section, containing new teeth, is moved up to replace it. However, there are some snails, known as cone shells, which have just a few very large teeth attached to their radula. These are hollow and barbed and the channel running through

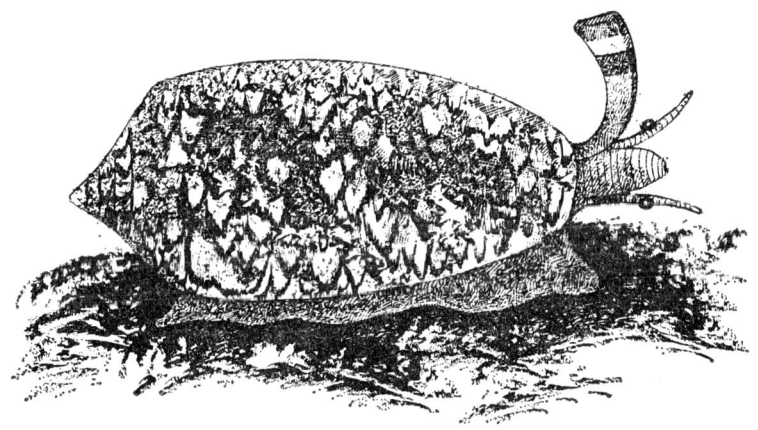

A cone shell snail. Cone shells have large teeth on their radula which are connected to poison glands as the diagram below shows.

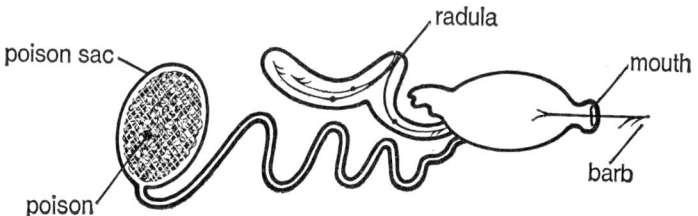

each tooth connects with a gland which produces one of the most venomous of all known animal toxins.

Incredibly, considering how slowly snails move, these cone shells all capture active prey, including marine worms and small fishes. They detect their prey not by sight but by smell, and glide towards it stealthily until within striking distance, having meantime protruded the proboscis through the mouth and erected one of the teeth into the striking position. The tooth is then suddenly buried in the flesh of the unsuspecting victim, and so quickly does the injected saliva work that the victim is paralysed before having any chance of shaking itself free.

Having made its capture the cone shell is faced with a problem: it has no array of minute teeth on the radula with which to scrape the prey into tiny pieces for swallowing. At the same time it cannot swallow the prey whole because the opening of the shell is only a narrow slit through which a whole worm or fish certainly could not pass. The problem is solved by the proboscis, which is capable of being stretched to engulf the whole prey. Within the proboscis digestive juices are poured over it, and the liquid products of digestion are then passed back through the mouth.

At least one species of cone shell, the Australian *Conus geographus*, has been responsible for a number of human deaths, and probably some other species could also be fatal to man.

Spiders

Spiders are the most universally venomous of all animals, surpassing even the snakes. Although there are large numbers of venomous snakes, there are even more whose saliva contains no toxin. But among the spiders there are only one or two small groups whose bite is not venomous, and these are the only ones capable of dealing with solid food. All the venomous kinds are only able to swallow liquids.

The spider's weapons consist of a pair of fangs on either side of the head. Each consists of two parts, a broad basal segment firmly fixed to the head and toothed along its inner edge, and a movable claw section which is curved and sharply pointed and has a tiny opening at its tip. When not in use the claw can be folded inwards against the toothed edge of the basal segment, rather like the blade of a penknife being folded into the handle. Within the head beneath each basal segment there is a gland filled with toxic liquid and surrounded by muscles, and from this gland a tube runs right through both segments of the fang to the opening at the tip of the claw. When a spider prepares to attack, it unfolds its fangs and then sinks them into its victim. At once the muscles surrounding the poison glands contract, so that the toxic fluid is forced into the wounds. The toxin it contains almost instantaneously paralyses and subsequently kills its prey.

Although there are so many venomous spiders, only a very few of them are dangerous to man. The best

POISON IN ANIMALS

known of these is the Italian tarantula, once thought to be the most deadly of all spiders to man, though we now know that it is not as dangerous as one or two other species. The tarantula is one of the wolf spiders – the spiders we see running about on the ground in our gardens, the female often carrying a whitish egg sac on her back.

The tarantula owes its name to the fact that it was first discovered near the Italian seaport of Taranto,

A diagram showing how the spider's fangs are connected to a poison gland within its head.

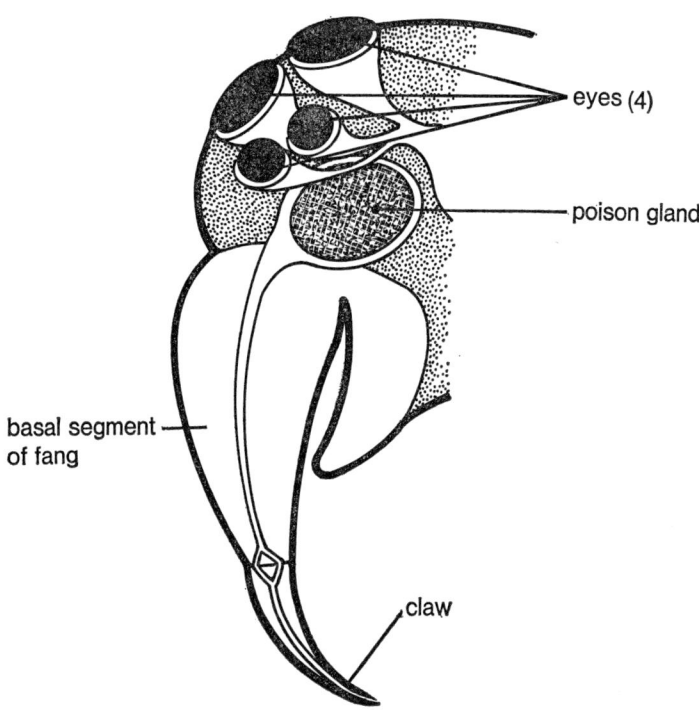

One kind of tarantula from South America can be as much as eighteen centimetres across and eats small birds. Even so, its bite is not dangerous to man.

and it has in its turn given its name to a type of musical composition known as the tarantella. A great deal of legend surrounds the effects of the bite of the tarantula. In earlier times it was said that the bite of the tarantula caused the victim to indulge in a frantic dance, which continued until he finally collapsed completely exhausted, but cured. The music of the tarantella was designed to accompany this frenzied dance. Another classic cure was to place the victim in a baker's oven, and for him to remain there until he could stand the heat no longer. We now know that the bite of the tarantula, while painful, and just possibly fatal to anyone suffering from acute heart disease, normally causes nothing more than intense pain for a few hours. After this the victim will recover just as well by undergoing

POISON IN ANIMALS

no treatment as by subjecting himself either to frenzied dancing or to the heat of the baker's oven.

Other spiders are more dangerous, and the most deadly of all is one known as *Atrax robustus* which lives in the Sydney area of Australia. The first known death from this spider, which belongs to the funnel-web group, was recorded in Sydney in 1927, and since then at least twelve people have died from *Atrax* bite. There must have been deaths before this, but they were probably wrongly blamed on poisonous snakes, of which there are plenty in Australia. The spiders make two neat punctures in the skin when they bite, and these look just like the punctures made by a snake bite.

Atrax robustus *emerging from its web.*

THE VENOMOUS BITE

The venom of these funnel-web spiders is extremely deadly, and great efforts have been made to produce an antidote serum. So far, however, these efforts have proved unsuccessful. One curious fact has emerged from these researches, which is that the venom of the male spider is about six times more poisonous than the venom of the female. Also it seems that people are much more likely to be bitten by males than by females. There is a good reason for this. Males move about in search of the females, which normally remain in their webs waiting for their mates to appear. During their search for females, too, the males may well come into houses, and thus into closer contact with people than the females are likely to do.

2
The Venomous Snakes

Most people regard snakes as dealers of death. In fact, however, many snakes are quite harmless, and only some groups are venomous. These venomous groups have a variety of methods of injecting their venom, and the ways in which the venom acts upon the victims also vary. Some toxins affect the nervous system, death being brought about by respiratory failure. These toxins are said to be neurotoxic. Other toxins destroy the cells of the blood and the blood-vessel linings. These are described as haemotoxic or haemorrhagic, and death is brought about by extensive internal bleeding. All snake venom consists of a mixture of both types of toxins, but in some groups one type predominates, while in other groups the other type predominates. A venomous snake's poison apparatus is fully formed and functional from the moment it is born or hatched, and although it may be only a few centimetres long it is nevertheless an extremely dangerous animal. Poison fangs do wear out, but in a venomous snake's jaws new fangs are always growing ready to replace those that are discarded.

This does not mean that everyone who is bitten dies. In many cases the snake does not manage to sink its fangs into the flesh, but merely grazes the skin, so that only a small amount of toxic saliva actually gets into the blood. This will probably be sufficient to cause severe pain and swelling, but not usually death. On many occasions, too, the salivary glands will contain little saliva because they have already been discharged some time before when the snake was capturing its last meal, and it takes at least some hours for the glands to be recharged. Today, too, serum injections save the lives of many who might otherwise die.

Even so it has been estimated that throughout the world something like 40,000 people die of snake bites every year, the largest proportion in Pakistan, India and elsewhere in South-East Asia. In India alone probably as many as 200,000 people are bitten each year, and of these some 15,000 die. But with few exceptions snakes prefer to avoid man rather than face up to him. Only when cornered, trodden, sat upon, or suddenly disturbed will most of them attempt to strike. Even then their apparent intention to strike is more often than not a bluff, and an actual strike will usually occur only if the person does not retreat. The one exception seems to be the king cobra, which has the reputation of actually advancing and attacking unprovoked.

Deadly though it is, one cannot but marvel at the speed and accuracy of the venomous snake's strike. It has been estimated that for a rattlesnake to strike, bite, inject venom into the wound under pressure, and to return to the initial position ready to strike again takes not more than half a second.

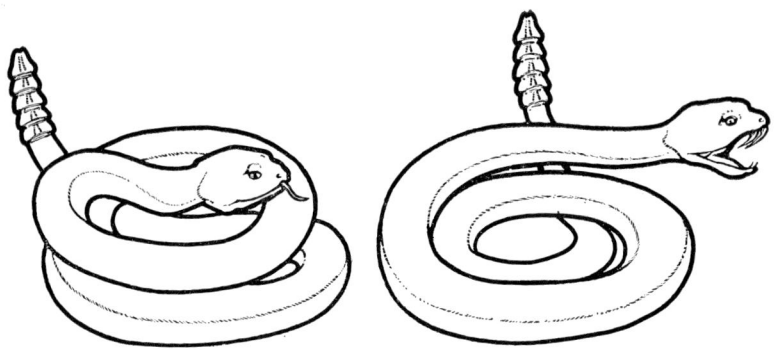

The rattlesnake can uncoil itself and strike in less than a second. It gets its name from the high-pitched rattle or buzz which the snake makes to warn off enemies.

The terrible potency of snake venom is well illustrated by an early experience of Frank Buckland, a distinguished nineteenth-century naturalist and writer. When quite a young man Buckland got hold of a rat that had just been killed by a cobra and proceeded to skin it. To get some of the flesh away from the skin he scraped it with his nails. About an hour before, he had been cleaning his nails with a penknife, and in doing so had slightly separated one nail from the quick. This crack was sufficient to allow a minute amount of the cobra venom to penetrate his blood. This was quite enough to make him so ill that for some time his chances of recovery were in doubt.

In Buckland's day no effective cure for snake bite was known. Indeed some of the curious and extravagant methods of treating a victim would have been more likely to hasten his end than to postpone it. Today, however, no one need die of snake bite if treatment is given promptly, thanks to the pioneer work of

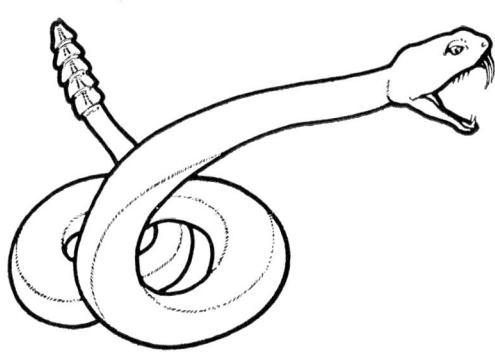

a Brazilian doctor and naturalist, Dr Vital Brazil, based on the idea of using the snakes themselves to cure the bites they inflict.

Dr Brazil's idea was to produce a serum which could be injected like those used to neutralize the poisons or toxins produced by diphtheria and other bacterial diseases. To prepare such a serum would require regular supplies of venom. Accordingly Dr Brazil set up his famous snake farm ten kilometres outside the city of São Paulo. Here hundreds of deadly snakes were kept, the collection representing every poisonous snake found in Brazil, so that venom was always to hand when required.

Every few days the snakes were 'milked' of their venom, an operation requiring both skill and courage. The snake was first gripped firmly by the back of the neck so that it could not reach its captor with its fangs. A small glass with a covering of sterilized gauze across the top was then brought towards the snake. Inevitably it would strike, being in a bad temper through being held. The hollow fangs pierced the gauze while a few drops of venom, forced through the cavity of the fangs, dripped into the glass.

The venom was then diluted, and minute amounts of the solution were injected into the horses and mules which were used in the preparation of the serum. Each animal was injected with the serum from only one species of snake. Repeated injections, gradually becoming stronger, over a period of some months stimulated the blood serum of these animals to produce substances called antitoxins, which neutralized the toxins in the snake venom and thereby rendered them harmless.

Once an animal had built up a good concentration of the antitoxins, it became a donor. It was, of course, a very valuable animal, and every possible care was taken of it. From now on it lived a life of comparative leisure and was well fed. Every so often a portion of its blood was withdrawn, the valuable serum containing the antitoxin being separated from the other blood constituents, sterilized and sealed in small tubes, each containing sufficient for the treatment of one snake-bite victim. These tubes were then distributed to medical and first-aid centres, to landowners and estate managers, and to doctors. They were thus readily available in any part of the country when needed. This was very important, because without serum treatment snake-bite victims soon die.

Each snake venom of course produces a serum effective only against bites from that particular species; and in countries like South America, Africa and India there are many different kinds of venomous snakes. So

THE VENOMOUS SNAKES

to be effective the injection given to someone bitten by a venomous snake must be the serum appropriate to the venom of that snake. One problem was quickly realized. Although there might be stocks of sera for all the venomous snakes living in the area, unless the victim could identify the particular species which had bitten him, serum treatment was impossible. And anyone bitten by a snake was unlikely to have examined his assailant carefully. Indeed he might not even have seen it.

This realization prompted Dr Brazil to turn his attention to the production of a universal serum which would be effective against any of them. To produce this serum would be a long and tedious process since it would be necessary to give the animal producing the serum a graded series of injections of each venom in turn. The complete course of injections in fact took about two years before the full composite serum was available.

The value and effectiveness of Dr Brazil's work is unquestionable. In the state of São Paulo alone, he was able to reduce an average death rate from snake bite from 250 to a rarity. One of the doctor's earliest and most spectacular triumphs occurred in New York, where he had gone to deliver a lecture explaining his work and its purpose, bringing along with him samples of his sera to illustrate his lecture.

While unpacking a rattlesnake newly arrived at New York Zoo, a keeper was severely bitten on the hand. Despite immediate first aid, the poor man was in a very serious condition by the time he had been rushed to hospital. Fortunately the hospital authorities remembered that Dr Brazil was in town, and in response to a frantic telephone call he hurried to the hospital, bringing with him his precious demonstration tubes of serum. One glance at the patient was sufficient to tell him that death was not far off. Without losing a moment, the doctor injected a full dose of serum. Within the hour the keeper had begun to improve, and eventually made a complete recovery.

Dr Brazil's work inspired other workers in other parts of the world to establish similar snake farms, where sera relating to their native poisonous snakes could be produced. Today snake sera are available for all the world's venomous snakes. All zoos which keep snakes carry stocks of serum to deal with bites from any of them.

Some people have the idea that in countries where venomous snakes are common you will always be running into them. Nothing could be farther from the truth. In fact it is possible to live for years in such a country without setting eyes on a snake. Snakes in fact are as keen to keep out of our way as we are to keep out of theirs. Those you are most likely to encounter are the ones that come into houses, and the greatest menace among these is the Indian cobra, which likes to come indoors and hide away in cosy corners.

Many accidents have occurred through people unknowingly disturbing these cobras in hiding, and there have been some miraculous escapes. The necessity for a cool head at these times was never better demonstrated than many years ago by an army officer serving

THE VENOMOUS SNAKES

in India. One day, while workmen were busy inside carrying out repairs to his bungalow, he was lying on the verandah with his shirt open, reading a book. It was a hot afternoon, and he soon fell asleep. Waking up later, he felt something cold lying on his chest under his open shirt. To his intense horror he saw that it was a cobra, curled up and apparently asleep. To move or to disturb it meant almost certain death. With tremendous courage and self-control he decided that the only thing to do was to lie perfectly still and hope that the snake might eventually glide away. For what must have seemed a lifetime he waited. Eventually he heard footsteps approaching. One of the workmen was coming out to speak to him. The cobra took fright and glided away, leaving the officer rather shattered in nerve, but otherwise unscathed.

Back-fanged snakes

More than half of all known snakes belong to a family known as the Colubridae, and in the majority of these the saliva lacks any kind of toxin. The victims are killed as a result of the wounds inflicted by the snakes' teeth. But some of the colubrids have developed a mildly toxic saliva, partly neurotoxic, partly haemotoxic, and the teeth at the back of the upper jaw have developed grooves down which this saliva is channelled into the wound that they have made. These back-fanged snakes, as they are called, are not very efficient poisoners, because in order to inject their toxic saliva they must be able to chew the flesh of their victims with the back teeth, and this is not easy to do unless the victim is very small. Only one of these back-fanged colubrids is at all dangerous to man, the African boomslang.

Front-fanged snakes

The most important front-fanged snakes are the cobras of Africa and Asia, the kraits of Asia, the mambas of Africa, the coral snakes of America and all the poisonous snakes of Australia, the most dangerous of which are the tiger snake and the death adder. The majority are slender and swift moving, and some grow to a considerable length. The longest of all is the king cobra or hamadryad of India and other parts of Asia, which can grow to a length of six metres.

All the front-fanged snakes are venomous and dangerous. The scientific name for these snakes is the Elapidae, but they are known as the front-fanged snakes because it is the teeth at the front of the upper jaws which have become grooved to carry the toxic saliva into the wound. In some species the edges of the grooves almost meet so that the grooves are nearly closed channels. The method which these snakes use to inject the venom is the strike. The head and front part of the body are raised from the ground, the mouth is opened wide and then aimed with great rapidity at the potential victim, the long fangs sinking into its flesh. As they do so muscles surrounding the salivary glands

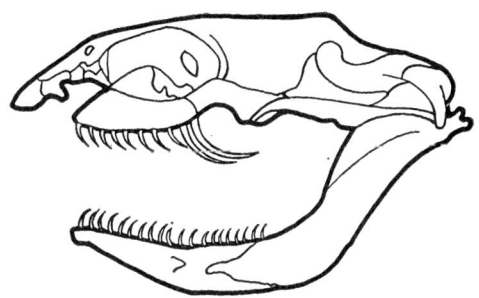

Diagrams showing the fangs of back-fanged snakes (top) and front-fanged snakes. With back-fanged snakes the venom usually paralyses the prey only as it is being swallowed, whereas front-fanged snakes use their large front fang to stab and poison at the same time.

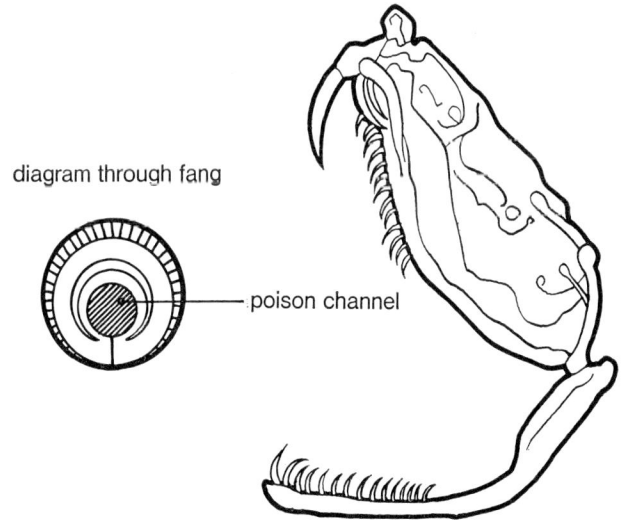

lying in the jaws above them are suddenly contracted and saliva flows down the grooves and into the wound. The toxins contained in the saliva are mainly neuro-

The black-necked cobra, also known as the spitting cobra. It spits poison at its enemy's eyes.

toxic. The fangs are quickly withdrawn to avoid any possible retaliation on the part of the victim. The strike is used to kill animals suitable to eat, and in defence if the snake is threatened with attack by an animal larger and stronger than itself.

Two African cobras, the ringhals and the black-necked cobra, are known as the spitting cobras because they are able to squirt a jet of venom a distance of over a metre with remarkable accuracy. If a larger animal is rash enough to attack one of these snakes, or even approach too near to one it has not seen, the jets will be directed into its eyes, causing intense pain and temporary blindness.

Sea snakes

Sea snakes are quite small, seldom exceeding one and a half metres in length, and their tails are flattened from side to side and used to propel them through the water. They are quite common in many parts of the Indian

Sea snakes are either dark above and light below (see the title-page for a picture), or ringed in black and green. They live only on eels and fish, but their venom is extremely powerful. However, they rarely harm fishermen.

and Pacific Oceans. Their venom has been shown to be among the most deadly produced by any snake, yet they are quite docile creatures and therefore not as dangerous as most other venomous snakes. Even where there are plenty of them about in inshore waters they never attack bathers, and when fishermen bring them up in their nets they are able to pick them out and drop them back into the sea without having to take any precautions.

Vipers

The Viperidae (or vipers) have only fangs, not teeth, and these are at the front of the mouth. They are connected to the salivary glands by a completely enclosed tube. Unlike the fangs of the elapids, they can be folded back along the upper jaw when they are not in use, and this has meant that they can grow much longer than the fixed fangs of the elapids. The fangs of even the largest elapids seldom exceed twelve millimetres in length, whereas viper fangs are often at least twenty-five millimetres long, enabling them to be sunk much further into a victim's body. The venom produced by vipers consists mainly of haemotoxic toxins, so death is usually from internal bleeding.

There are two groups of vipers. There are those which live in the Old World, notably Russell's viper in Asia, the puff adder and the gaboon viper in Africa, and the British and European adder. The other group consists of the New World vipers. These are known as

Russell's viper lives chiefly in India, where it is much feared. It hunts at night and will even follow mice and rats into houses.

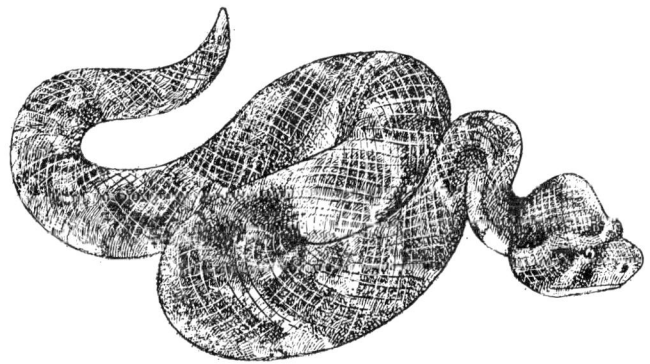

The puff adder is one of the largest vipers, and can inflate its body to double its size when disturbed.

The gaboon viper, found only in Africa.

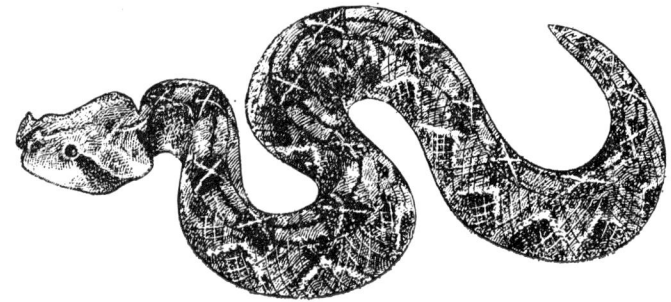

pit vipers because on each side of the head between the eye and the nostril there is a tiny pit. This is a remarkable sense organ for detecting heat rays, and enables the snake to detect the presence of warm-blooded prey in the dark by means of the infra-red rays given off by their bodies. It can thus hunt at night. The best known pit vipers are the rattlesnakes, the moccasins, the copperheads, the fer-de-lance and the bushmaster, which with a maximum length of four metres is the largest of all the Viperidae.

The European adder is found throughout Europe, and is the only viper in Britain. It is a dangerous snake since it is always ready to strike, and any bite should be treated immediately.

The fer-de-lance is common in Central America and some of the West Indian islands, where it has been known to attack workers on the sugar plantations.

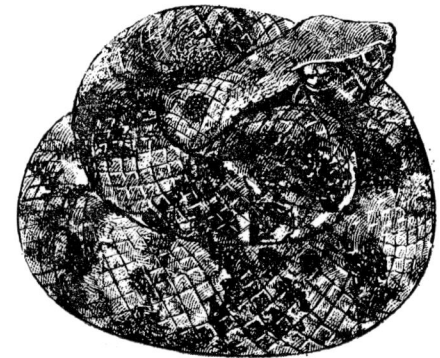

3
Poison Spines and Hairs

Teeth and jaws are just one of the ways in which poisons can be injected into a victim. Spines and hairs are also used. Poison spines are particularly favoured by a number of sea creatures. Like poison teeth and jaws, they are connected to glands which produce the toxic substances introduced into the victim's flesh when it is penetrated by the spines.

The wounds caused by the spines of venomous fish are extremely painful and sometimes also dangerous, but surprisingly none of them use their spines to kill their prey, merely to deter attackers. In fact they all live on easily obtained defenceless animals. And even for defence, a much milder and less painful toxin would probably be equally effective.

Similarly, sea-urchins, their body bristling with sharp spines, look sufficiently protected against attack. Yet quite a number of sea-urchin species do have the additional protection of a poison spine or curious pincer-like organs known as pedicellariae.

Hairs are used to inject poison by a few species of moth caterpillars. Many moths have hairy caterpillars, and their hairs provide them with a good deal of protection, because most predators are not keen to swallow anything hairy. A few of these hairy caterpillars, however, bear more than just unpleasant hairs. Among each tuft of relatively soft hairs there are also some barbed irritant bristles or spicules, capable of penetrating the skin of man or any other animal coming in contact with them.

Weever fish

The lesser weever or sting fish, a small European fish about fifteen centimetres long, feeds mainly on shrimps. It is widely distributed in inshore waters from the North Sea to the Mediterranean. Shrimps live on the sandy bottom just offshore, usually burying themselves just beneath the surface of the sand, out of which they are coaxed by the special nets used by shrimp fishermen. When it is not feeding on the shrimp the weever also wriggles into the surface layers of the sand, leaving its eyes and the tip of its specially upturned mouth protruding but inconspicuous.

The dorsal fin carries between five and seven black-tipped spines and their tips also project just above the surface. Being black, they are quite conspicuous against the pale colour of the sand. This, it is thought, may serve as a warning to other fish to keep clear of danger, and thus protect the weever from attack by these fish just as the warning black and yellow colouring of the wasp protects it from attack by birds and other insect-eating animals. The lesser weever also has another poisonous spine projecting backwards from each of the gill covers. All of these spines are needle-

The eyes of the weever fish are found on top of the head so they stick out above the sand when the fish buries itself. The lesser and greater weever are the most venomous fish in the North Sea.

sharp at their tips, and grooved, and near the tip of each spine there is a venom gland which discharges its toxic contents into the groove whenever the spine pierces the flesh of any other animal, including man.

Professional shrimp fishermen always wear boots to protect their feet when fishing, but they are also at risk when sorting their catch. If they discover a weever and pick it out, it will flex its body and flare out its gill covers in an attempt to bury its spines into its captor's flesh. The effects of the weever's spines can be very serious. They have recently been described in the following rather horrific terms: 'headache, fever, chills, delirium, nausea, vomiting, dizziness, joint aches, loss of speech, slow heartbeat, palpitation, mental depression, convulsions, difficulty in breathing and even death'.

The closely related greater weever, which is about twice the size of the lesser weever, is just as venomous as the smaller species but is not so dangerous because it is much less likely to be encountered. It is, however, often brought up in the fishermen's nets, and great care has to be taken to avoid handling it when the catch is being sorted.

A sting ray. These fish, like the weevers, spend a lot of their time in the sand with only their eyes and tail not buried. Their spines have sometimes been used to make daggers and spears.

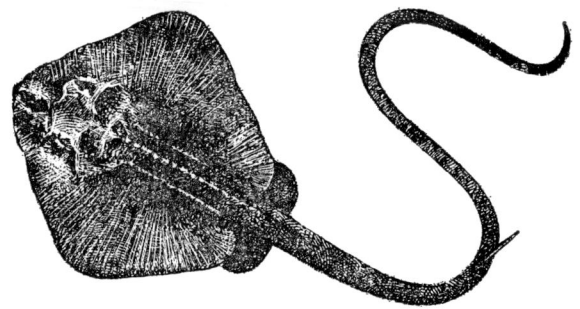

Sting ray

Sting rays are flat fish with, as their name suggests, a venomous spine or 'sting'. The tail of a sting ray is thick and whip-like, and it carries a single poison spine which is long, serrated and very sharp. This is capable of inflicting a deep jagged wound. The fish is very dangerous to handle, for if it is picked up it will lash its tail in an attempt to bury the spine in its attacker's flesh. Two grooves run throughout its length and along them lie the glands which secrete a venom sufficiently

POISON SPINES AND HAIRS

potent to kill a man. Like some snake venoms it acts on the nervous system. The spine, which may grow to a length of up to forty-five centimetres, is periodically shed and replaced by a new one which has been developing behind it. Sometimes three spines in different stages of development may be present at the same time.

Dragon fish

The dragon fish, also sometimes known as the lion fish or the fireworks fish, is easily the most beautiful of all

The beautiful, but dangerous, dragon fish lives chiefly in the Pacific Ocean.

the venomous fish. With its strikingly striped body and fins it does look rather fearsome – it is quite a common shallow-water species in tropical and subtropical regions, and is often found in shore rock pools. All along its back it has a series of large spines representing its dorsal fins. These are sharp-pointed and hollow, and at the base of each one there is a poison gland. Most venomous fish do not attack unless they are picked up, but if anyone approaches a dragon fish too closely it will raise its venomous spines, draw even closer and then turn on its side. If these obviously threatening moves are ignored it will suddenly hurl its body towards the intruder and bury its spines in his

A stonefish lurking at the bottom of the sea.

flesh, while at the same time the muscles surrounding the poison glands contract and send the venom through the hollow spines and into the wound.

Stonefish

The stonefish is the most dangerous of all venomous fish. It is an extremely ugly creature covered with warty growths on the skin which act as camouflage,

making it very difficult to be seen as it lies motionless on a rock. It does indeed look rather like just another piece of stone or rock, as its name implies. Normally it seldom moves, getting sufficient food just by waiting for crabs and other small animals which approach close enough to be engulfed in its very large mouth. Even if it is prodded it is very difficult to persuade it to move.

Although it is not in the least aggressive it is extremely well armoured. Along its back it has thirteen very strong grooved spines with a venom gland at the base of each one opening into the groove. Normally these spines lie along the surface of the back, but if danger threatens they can be raised to a vertical position. They are quite capable of penetrating a thick rubber sole if they are trodden on. In addition to these dorsal spines it has three more beneath the body forming part of the anal fin, and one on each of the paired hind fins. The pain caused by stonefish venom is said to be almost unbearable, worse perhaps than the pain caused by any other animal poison. It can result in the loss of the poisoned limb, and sometimes even death.

Sea-urchins

Among the most beautiful of sea-urchins are various species of *Diadema*. They have quite a small body, but their spines are long, thin and movable, with light and dark horizontal banding. If anything, including a human foot, comes down towards them from above

A Diadema *sea-urchin. Its long, thin spines are very sensitive to light. In some species a slight shadow falling across the animal will cause the spines to point in the direction of whatever caused it.*

there is a rapid response, and all the spines are moved so that their tips point towards the impending danger. These spines are barbed, and like the spines of all sea-urchins they are covered with a thin layer of cells, but in this case some of the cells are glandular, producing a mildly poisonous irritant substance. If someone steps on a *Diadema*, that part of each spine which penetrates the foot becomes broken off because the barbs prevent it from being withdrawn. At the same time the glandular cells burst to release their contents into the wound, causing considerable pain. Over a period of days or weeks, depending upon the species, the spines are gradually dissolved in the victim's blood, and the pain subsides.

Much more to be feared, however, is another species called *Asthenosoma varium*. In contrast to *Diadema* its spines are quite short, but near the tip of each there is a blue-coloured poison sac. As soon as the spine penetrates flesh this sac contracts and forces the poison into the wound under pressure. This species occurs quite commonly in the offshore waters in which the Japanese pearl fishermen work, and is dreaded by them for contact with one of them can put a fisherman out of action for weeks while he makes a painful recovery.

Both sea-urchins and their relatives, the starfish, have curious pincer-like organs known as pedicellariae scattered all over the surface of the body. Normally

A sea-urchin. The largest sea-urchin ever found (in Japan) measured only about thirty centimetres across, and most specimens are much smaller than that, but some species are still painful to touch.

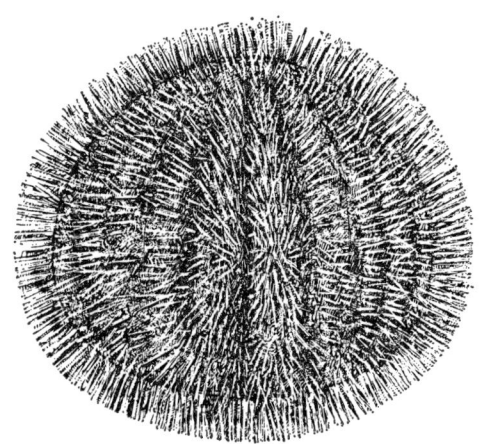

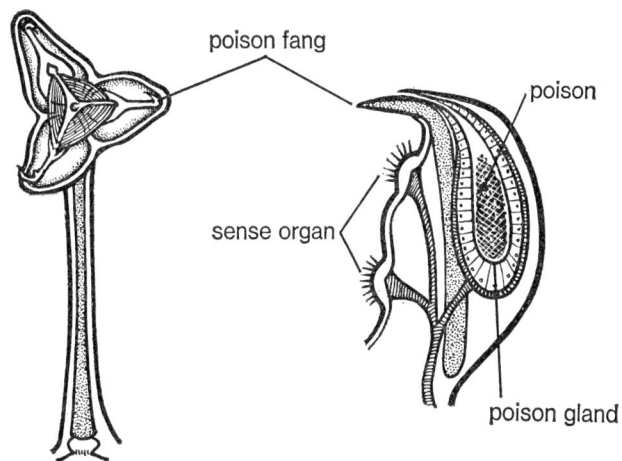

Left: a pedicellaria shown in its normal position with the three valves open, when it looks like a tiny flower. Right: a cross-section through one of the valves shows the sharp incurved fang connected to a poison gland.

they are used to pick up and dispose of any tiny unwanted particles which may fall on the skin, thus preventing the animal from being gradually covered with debris. Mostly these pedicellariae measure only about a millimetre or so in width.

One group of sea-urchins has venomous pedicellariae. These are various species of *Toxopneustes*, and like the other venomous sea-urchins they occur mainly in tropical waters. Each of the special poisonous pedicellariae consists of three sections or valves which can either be opened out to look like a tiny three-petalled flower, or closed up together like a flower bud. The base of each valve is thickened and contains a poison gland, while the tip forms an extremely sharp incurved fang which is hollow and carries a channel leading up

POISON IN ANIMALS

from the poison gland. Normally the three valves are held in the open position, but as soon as anything touches one of these pedicellariae the muscles connecting the valves contract and the three fangs are rapidly closed and buried into the flesh of the intruder. As they do so the muscles surrounding the poison glands also contract and the poison is forced under pressure through the perforated fang into the wound. Although they are so small these poisonous pedicellariae are very potent.

A Japanese biologist picked up one of these sea-urchins and was stung by only about half a dozen of its pedicellariae. But the poison he received was sufficient to cause intense pain, giddiness, difficulty in breathing

This specimen of a Pycnopodia *has twenty arms – the number of arms which most starfish have is usually a multiple of five.*

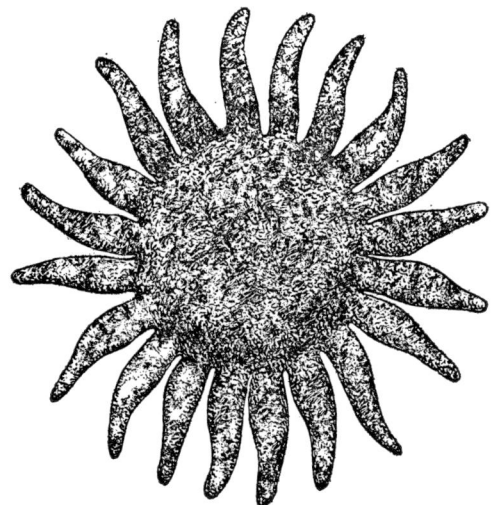

and partial paralysis of the face muscles, and it was some hours before he returned to normal. Since an individual *Toxopneusta* carries many hundreds of these globiferous pedicellariae, full contact with a specimen could obviously produce very serious results, and perhaps even death.

There is one kind of starfish, *Pycnopodia*, with pedicellariae capable of producing painful wounds. It lives in shallow waters off the west coast of North America.

Yellow-tail and brown-tail moth

The yellow-tail moth is white, with a tuft of yellow hair surrounding the hind end of the body, but its caterpillars are more striking in appearance, being mainly black with white and red markings. Tufts consisting of both normal hairs and spicules are arranged along each side of the body. If one of these caterpillars is touched some of its spicules penetrate the skin and inject a strongly irritant substance which causes pain considerably worse than that caused by contact with a stinging nettle.

When fully grown the yellow-tail caterpillar spins a cocoon or chrysalis case within which it will undergo all the changes which will convert it from a caterpillar to an adult moth. Before embarking on this metamorphosis, however, it sheds its final larval skin, and with it of course the hairs and spicules. Eventually the young adult moth is fully formed and ready to emerge from the chrysalis case. If it is a male moth it just breaks out of the chrysalis case, expands and dries its wings, and then flies away.

If it is a female, however, before she flies away she sweeps over the old larval skin with her tuft of yellow hairs, picking up a large number of the caterpillar hairs and spicules. When she subsequently mates and lays eggs these become covered with a layer of these hairs and spicules as they pass out of her body. These spicules provide the developing eggs with a considerable degree of protection, because most would-be predators prefer to leave them alone rather than risk a painful sting. The male does not collect up spicules because he will not be laying eggs. A female, of course, must also be handled carefully, keeping clear of her hair tufts.

The caterpillar of the brown-tail moth also has poisonous spicules. These caterpillars are black with

A brown-tail moth caterpillar.

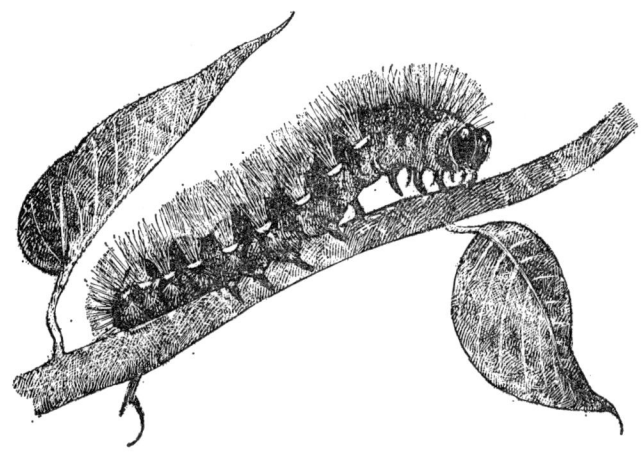

POISON SPINES AND HAIRS

two lines of white markings down the back and two bright orange spots between them towards the front end of the body. You are more likely to brush against these caterpillars than those of the yellow-tail because they congregate in large numbers on bramble and blackthorn bushes in the spring. At night they retire to communal webs, dispersing all over the bushes during the daytime to feed. The adult moth is similar in appearance to the yellow-tail, but its tuft of hairs at the hind end of the body is dark brown in colour.

4
Microscopic Sting Cells

Sea anemones, jellyfish and their relatives form a group known as the coelenterates. They are among the most primitive of all living animals. Their bodies are jelly-like and they have no jaws or teeth or other hard parts with which they could capture and cut up prey. Yet they are carnivorous, and are capable of killing quite large active animals.

Sea anemones

The body of a sea anemone consists of a hollow cylinder with a cavity opening only at one end. This cavity is the stomach, and the single opening the mouth, which is surrounded by a large number of tentacles that wave about in the water like slender fingers. If you watch an anemone in a rock pool you may be lucky enough to see a prawn or a small fish swim past close enough to brush against some of its tentacles. You will not see anything happen, and the anemone makes no movement. Yet the prawn or fish will stop dead in its tracks. It may struggle a bit, but is unable to break away, and in a short time it will be dead, and apparently attached in some invisible way to the tentacles. These now bend

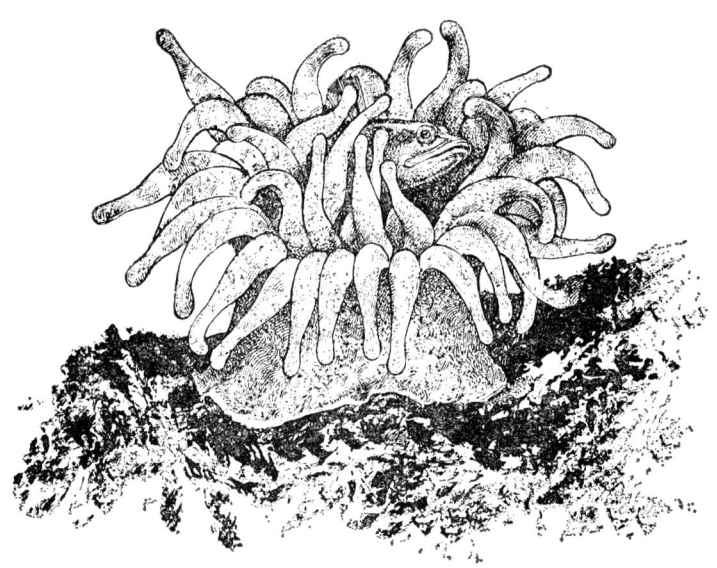

A fish trapped inside a sea anemone.

inwards towards the anemone's mouth, passing the dead prey through it into the stomach.

Only with the aid of a microscope can we find out what caused this apparently mysterious death. Among the surface cells of the anemone tentacles there are large numbers of sting cells. Inside each one is an oval capsule known as a nematocyst. This contains a poisonous fluid as well as a barbed harpoon at the end of a coiled thread which is fixed to the nematocyst wall. Projecting from the surface of the sting cell itself is a minute trigger-like object. When this is touched by the body of any small passing animal it causes the nematocyst to burst open and the harpoon to be shot out to penetrate the skin of the prey. In doing so of course it carries some of the poison into the wound. Because the sting cells are so minute and there are so many of them,

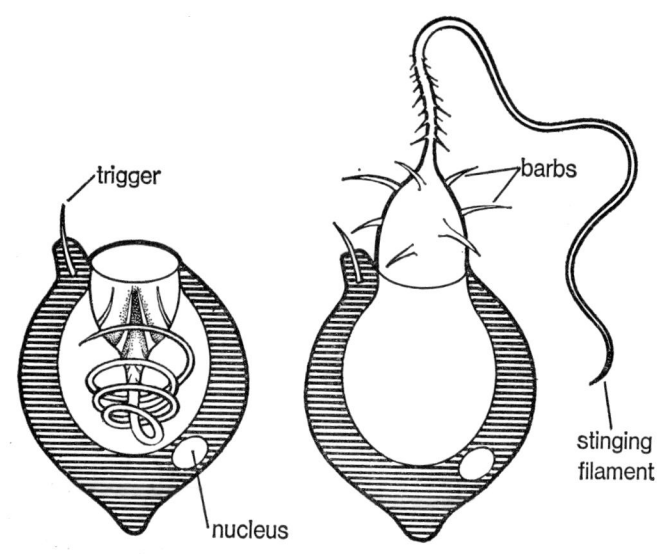

How a sea anemone's sting cells work: when the trigger is touched a long filament (or harpoon) is shot out at the passing animal. These pictures show the sting cell before (left) and after firing.

the slightest touch will release large numbers of harpoons, and these collectively will inject a considerable amount of poison into the body of the victim. This poison is of the neurotoxic kind, and kills by nerve paralysis. The harpoon threads remain attached to the nematocyst wall, so the prey is firmly held by the tentacles as they carry it to the anemone's mouth. The poison is not dangerous to man, but people with sensitive skins can get a stinging sensation when they touch the tentacles of certain species. It is rather like a mild form of the sting produced by touching a stinging nettle, and similar white lumps may develop for an hour or two.

On the coral reefs around many of the Pacific islands, including the Great Barrier Reef off the east

MICROSCOPIC STING CELLS

coast of Australia, there are a number of very large sea anemones, and associated with them are a similar number of highly coloured fish variously known as coral fish, damsel fish or clown fish. The remarkable thing about these fish is that they are able to live among the tentacles of the anemones without coming to any harm. It was thought at one time that these fish were naturally immune to the poison, but we now know that a much more complicated relationship exists between the anemones and their attendant fish. The fish have to train the anemones to accept them without killing them.

Each individual fish has to establish its own association with its chosen anemone. If it just swam straight into the circle of tentacles it would be killed at once and eaten. Instead it first swims close to the anemone and just brushes against the end of one or perhaps a few tentacles. This produces a violent reaction on the part of the anemone, and the discharge of nematocysts from the areas which have been touched. The fish frees itself with a violent jerk. The number of nematocysts it has received are not sufficient to do it any harm. It now returns, and this time it makes contact with more tentacles. More nematocysts are discharged, but the reaction of the anemone is less violent than it was the first time. Over a period of about an hour the fish makes repeated contact with the anemone, each time moving further into the mass of tentacles, and each time provoking less and less response until eventually it is able to settle itself right in the middle of the tentacles without a single nematocyst being discharged.

POISON IN ANIMALS

What has happened is that the anemone's nematocysts have become acclimatized to a certain substance contained in the mucus covering the fish's body. From now on the fish can leave the anemone and swim off to catch its food and subsequently return without any danger of triggering off its nematocysts, but if any other fish, even one of the same species, swims among the anemone's tentacles it will be killed and eaten.

This relationship between anemones and coral fish is an interesting example of commensalism, the name given to a partnership between two quite different kinds of animal in which both benefit. The fish gain great protective advantage, for their potential enemies are unlikely to attack them while they are lying among the anemone tentacles, because they would be killed and eaten by the anemone. What advantage the anemone gains is not quite so clear. Perhaps it obtains food: when the fish swims out and returns with captured prey, the anemone picks up pieces which the fish drops as it eats. Sometimes, too, the anemone may catch and eat any fish which may be chasing its partner as it returns to the safety of the tentacles. Whatever the truth may be there is plenty of evidence that anemones with coral fish partners do seem to thrive more than those without partners.

Because of their nematocysts, most animals avoid attacking sea anemones. One group of animals, the sea slugs, do however feed on them. They are immune to the nematocysts because for some unexplained reason they are able to eat the tentacles without discharging them, so that they reach the slug's stomach intact.

Even then they are not discharged. Instead they work their way through the body until they come to lie in special swellings along the back of the slug. Here they provide a very effective deterrent to any would-be enemies of the slug, because if the slug is attacked the nematocysts are discharged into the body of the predator. The slugs are thus protected by weapons borrowed from the anemones.

Common jellyfish

Jellyfish float free in the sea, travelling where the currents take them, for they have only limited means of propelling themselves through the water. With its mouth facing downwards and its flattened body, the jellyfish looks like an umbrella or an inverted saucer. It has tentacles carrying sting cells surrounding its mouth or suspended around the edge of the umbrella. The jellyfish you are most likely to bump into when you are swimming is the common jellyfish *Aurelia*, which can be found in almost any part of the world. Large specimens may have a diameter of about half a

The common jellyfish – Aurelia.

metre. Contact with its tentacles can be painful – like falling into a bed of stinging nettles – but not dangerous.

Sea wasp

The sea wasp is the most venomous of all jellyfish, and perhaps the most dangerous of all venomous animals that live in the sea. It occurs in considerable numbers along the coast of Queensland in Australia and on the offshore Barrier Reef in this area. Unlike *Aurelia* its bell is not circular but square, and about eight centimetres across. A single tentacle hangs down from each of the four corners. During the twenty-five years up to 1970 no fewer than sixty people were killed as a result of being stung by sea wasps in the Queensland area. During the same period man-eating sharks, which are generally regarded as extremely dangerous all down the east coast of Australia, accounted for only thirteen deaths. Sea wasp venom works very fast. Cases have been recorded in which the victim has died within minutes of being stung.

Portuguese man-of-war

Next to the sea wasp, the Portuguese man-of-war is the most dangerous of all the coelenterates. It is found all round the world, being absent only from the coldest polar seas. At first sight it looks like a jellyfish with a considerable number of long trailing tentacles. These tentacles, though, are not hanging down from an umbrella, but are attached to an air-filled float surmounted by a crest which acts as a sail. This float may be up to thirty centimetres long in a large specimen, and is an attractive blue in colour.

Although a Portuguese man-of-war may look something like a jellyfish, it is not an individual animal but a colony consisting of a large number of individuals living together. These are of several different kinds, and they are all suspended from the under surface of the rigid float. Some of them are specialized to do all the eating and digesting of food not only for themselves but for the rest of the colony as well. Others catch the colony's food. From these, tentacles, up to ten metres in length and furnished with enormous numbers of sting cells, hang down into the water. As the wind catching the sail drives the colony along, these tentacles trail out behind. If one of them touches a fish the extremely venomous nematocysts are discharged and the fish is captured. It is then drawn upwards by the shortening of the tentacles and handed over to the feeding individuals to deal with.

Because they have no power of movement themselves, but are at the mercy of the winds, Portuguese men-of-war are often driven ashore. If you should see even one floating on the sea when you are swimming, make for the shore at once. Contact with its tentacles causes instant and almost unbearable pain, followed by intestinal pains, vomiting and sometimes even partial paralysis and collapse. It takes several days to

POISON IN ANIMALS

recover. Deaths have occurred, mainly among children, but contact is also extremely dangerous for an adult with a weak heart. If you find a specimen washed up on the beach don't touch it even though it may appear to be quite dead. Its nematocysts are still able to be discharged by contact.

The Portuguese man-of-war is dangerous to man and most fish, but there is one small fish in the Gulf of Mexico which lives among its tentacles without being hurt. For obvious reasons, this is known as the Portuguese man-of-war fish. Their ability to live together is like that of the anemone and coral fish described on pp. 57–8.

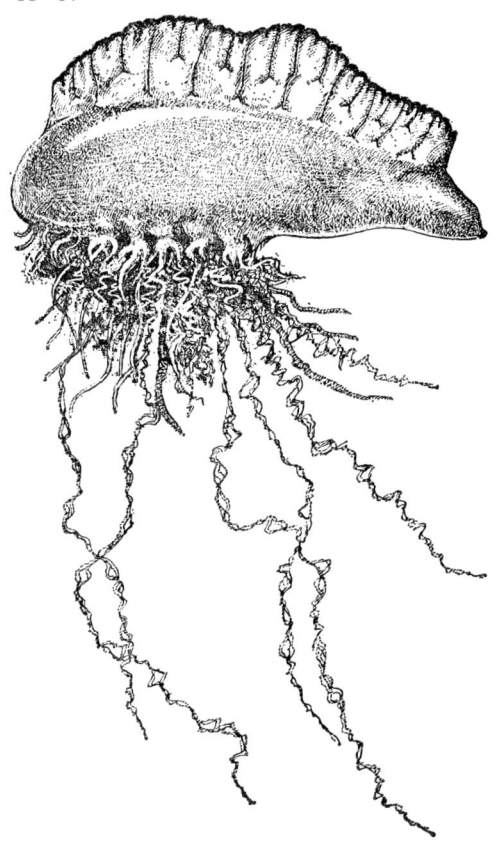

5
Poisoning by Sting

The word 'sting' is used to describe any structure situated at the hind end of an animal and capable of injecting venom into a victim. It is one of the most efficient methods devised by nature to inject poison and, besides the scorpions, is found only among insects. But this does not mean that all insects sting. Of the twenty-nine or so groups or orders into which the vast kingdom of the insects is divided, only one order contains insects which can sting, the order Hymenoptera. And not all of these possess a sting, only the bees, ants and wasps.

The origin of these insects' stings is rather curious. The egg duct of insects opens at the hind tip of the abdomen, and in many insects it is prolonged into a hollow tube known as the ovipositor, through which the egg travels before it is deposited, often on a leaf or in the ground. In the bees, ants and wasps this ovipositor has become modified as a sting, and what now passes down the hollow tube is not the egg, but venom produced by poison glands situated inside the body. Eggs now pass out through an opening at the base of the ovipositor. Of course, since only female insects produce eggs and possess an ovipositor, it is only the females which are capable of stinging. So male bees, ants and wasps are quite harmless.

Bees

A colony or a hive of bees, whether honey bees or bumble bees, contains three kinds of individuals. The queens are fertile females which do all the egg-laying. The workers are sterile females which do all the collecting of nectar and pollen on which the adult bees and the grubs are fed, as well as all the work of the hive. Both possess a sting. The males, or drones as they are called, contribute nothing to the upkeep of the colony, though they do feed on the food which the workers bring in. Their sole function is to mate with virgin queens on their nuptial flight. Since they are males they have no sting.

A bee's sting consists of three parts. One of these is a grooved channel in which the other two parts lie. These are sharp lancets barbed near their tips. The

A worker bee.

whole sting, when not in use, is withdrawn into a special sting-chamber at the hind end of the abdomen. Since bees feed on plant products they do not kill animals as prey. The sting is used purely defensively. If a queen or a worker bee is picked up by man or by any other animal, the sting is protruded and its tip aimed at the aggressor. As soon as the first lancet penetrates the skin it is held in place by its backwardly directed barbs so that it cannot be withdrawn. Meanwhile, the second lancet also penetrates the skin and is similarly held. A rapid alternation of movement sinks the barbed lancets deeper and deeper into the skin of the victim, while at the same time venom is forced into the wound down the grooved channel. All this takes place in a mere fraction of a second. Unfortunately for the bee, when it flies off, the whole of its poison apparatus is torn out from its abdomen, and it soon dies.

The amount of venom introduced by a bee sting is very small, less than half a milligram, yet it can cause considerable distress and swelling of the surrounding tissue. Even today the composition of bee venom is not known, but it is thought that the sting injects the products of three distinct glands. One produces a substance which acts as lubricant, making the movements of the lancets easier, while the other two produce an acid and an alkaline fluid, all three being mixed together to produce the complete venom as they pass down the grooved channel.

Beekeepers believe that regular stinging by bees can act as a preventive or a cure for rheumatism. Science is not sure. Certainly, remarkable results are sometimes

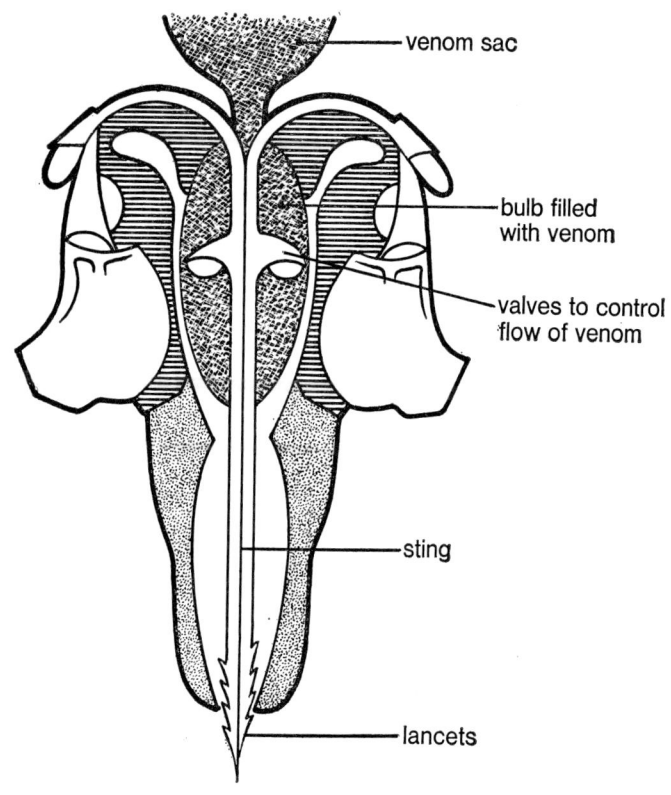

A diagram of the special sting chamber on the bee's abdomen.

achieved when a patient suffering from rheumatism allows himself to be stung repeatedly by bees. But in other cases no benefit seems to result. Further research is needed to find out whether bee venom can have any beneficial medical use. In fact, bee venom in large quantities can be fatal. In tropical countries wild bees build enormous nests, and if one of these is disturbed the bees will come out and attack the intruder, who may well be killed by multiple stinging.

Ants

Ants use stings less than bees, and whether they have a sting or not, is related to their feeding habits. Some kinds of ant are hunters, killing other animals for food, and these generally have stings which they can use to kill their prey. Unlike bees, therefore, their stings represent aggressive rather than defensive weapons. An exception is the wood ant, which kills prey with its powerful jaws but has no sting. Other ants either feed on seeds or nectar, or on honey dew which they obtain by milking aphids or scale insects, or they cultivate fungi as food. The members of these groups are generally devoid of stings, though many of them are able to squirt formic acid as a defensive weapon at any predators which threaten to attack them.

The red ant (left) and black ant are just two of the forty-seven species of ant found in Britain. All these species feed on honey dew. The red ant possesses a sting, but this is used to deal with enemies – like nest invaders – rather than to kill prey.

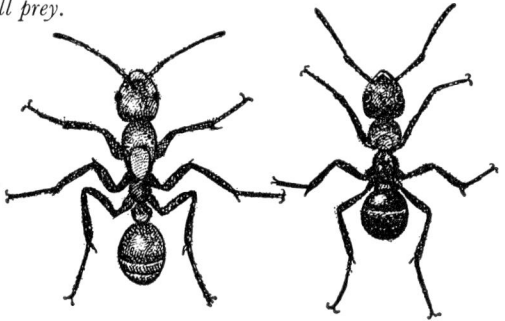

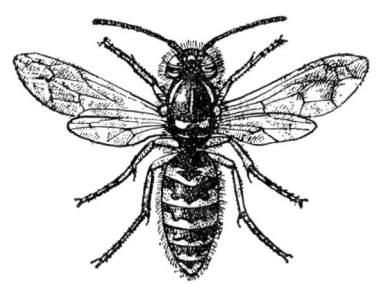

A worker wasp.

Common wasps

The common wasps are social insects like bees and ants, living in large colonies or nests. Although the adults live mainly on nectar and other plant juices – they are very fond of ripe fruit – their grubs are completely carnivorous, and while they are growing the workers have to bring in to the nest a steady supply of dead insects and other small animals. These are caught and killed by the workers' powerful jaws. The sting, which they all possess, is used entirely as a defensive weapon. Wasps are much more ready to sting than bees, probably because the wasp can withdraw its sting without damaging itself. This is not, as many people believe, because the wasp sting lancets are not barbed. They are, but the barbs are much smaller than those of a bee sting, and do not prevent the sting being withdrawn.

Solitary wasps

Although the social wasps are the ones we are most familiar with, they represent only a minority of the wasps. The majority are solitary wasps, and these have the most remarkable method of feeding their young. There are no worker solitary wasps to collect food for growing grubs, only males and fertile females, the two sexes coming together only briefly to mate. The future grubs are provided with a store of food sufficient for their entire larval needs at the time the egg is laid. The female does this by seeking out a suitable insect or other small animal and stinging it. It is not killed, however, but permanently paralysed. It is then taken to the place where the egg is laid, and shut in with it. As soon as the egg hatches, the tiny grub begins to feed on this fresh meat that its mother has provided for it.

There are three main types of solitary wasp, each with its own nesting and provisioning habits. These are the spider wasps, which are the most primitive group, the sand or digger wasps, and the mason or potter wasps, which are related to the true social wasps. After mating in the late spring or early summer, the female spider wasp immediately starts searching for her spider prey. It may be a species which lives in a burrow or a web, but in either case the wasp first chases it from its home, and grabs it from behind so as to keep clear of its poison fangs. It then curls its abdomen round beneath the spider's abdomen and stings it, paralysis occurring almost immediately. Although spiders, as we have already seen, are themselves well armed, they seem to be panic-stricken at the approach of one of these wasps, for they apparently make no attempt to defend themselves.

Spider wasps live in areas where the soil is sandy and

A spider wasp stinging its prey. There are many different kinds of spider wasp, and the largest – from Central America – can be up to forty millimetres long.

therefore soft and easily excavated. They also occur on sand dunes. As soon as she has captured her spider, the female wasp hides it as best she can while she searches for a suitable spot where she can excavate a burrow a few centimetres deep. While she is doing this, she may break off on several occasions and return for a moment to her prey, presumably making sure that it has not been stolen by some other predator. When she has finally completed her burrow, she returns again to the spider, grabs hold of it and drags it behind her to the nest; this is no mean feat since the spider may well be as large as she is. When she reaches her burrow, she leaves the spider on the rim and enters head first. Then she turns round, drags the spider down to the bottom, lays an egg on its under side and crawls out. Finally, the hole is filled in to prevent other predators finding the egg with its paralysed prey. Having constructed and stocked one nest, she now goes in search of another victim, repeating the whole process a number of times until she has used up her complete stock of fertilized eggs. She never returns to these nests, leaving the grubs to grow and pupate without any parental

POISONING BY STING

attention. Soon after laying the last of her eggs she dies.

The sand wasps also construct their burrows in light, sandy soils, but, in common with all solitary wasps other than spider wasps, the nest is constructed first. After mating, the female searches for a suitable site for her nest, often examining a number of sites before she is satisfied. Having found a site, she excavates a vertical shaft about two or three centimetres deep, and then continues to burrow horizontally, this second part of the burrow ending in an oval nest chamber. While she is digging she leaves the nest periodically and flies around in all directions over it, as if trying to remember surrounding landmarks so that she can find it

A female sand wasp carrying a paralysed caterpillar back to her nest. As the picture shows, this consists of a small shaft, then a tunnel leading to a chamber.

again later after it has been stocked and filled in. As we shall see, unlike most other solitary wasps, she does return repeatedly to her nest.

Once she is finally satisfied that the nest is finished, she goes off in search of suitable food with which to stock it. This is always a caterpillar which she first paralyses by stinging, and then drags to the nest. Once she has managed to deposit it in the nest chamber she lays an egg on it. Then she leaves the nest, filling in the entrance with loose soil before flying away. After a few days she returns and opens up the nest. By this time the grub will have hatched and started feeding on the caterpillar. The purpose of the return visit is to see whether the grub has finished the first caterpillar and is ready for more food. If it is, she flies off and returns with another one. From now on she will visit the nest each day, usually in the morning, fetching a fresh caterpillar whenever she finds that the previous one has been eaten. This continues until the grub has reached full size and is ready to pupate. She now leaves the nest for the last time. Sometimes a female may excavate two and occasionally three nests. Continual stocking of more than one nest certainly keeps the female busy.

The mason, or potter, wasps are so called because, instead of excavating a nest chamber, they actually construct little vase-shaped cells made of earth, hanging them from twigs of heather or other small shrubs. As soon as the female has finished her nest, leaving a small opening through which she can pass in or out, she sets about provisioning it. Whereas other kinds of

A potter wasp and its nest.

solitary wasps are content to supply their future offspring with a single paralysed victim at a time, the potter wasp collects a number of small caterpillars, piling them up until they nearly fill the nest. Only now does she lay her single egg, not on the prey like other solitary wasps but suspended from the ceiling by a thin thread so that it is just above the caterpillar on top of the pile. She then, finally, leaves the nest and seals up the exit hole.

When the tiny grub hatches, it eats the top caterpillar while remaining suspended by the thread. Only then does it detach itself and drop on to the remaining caterpillars, which it proceeds to eat one by one. As in all the solitary wasps, the amount of food provided by the female is always just enough to enable the grub to grow to full size and become ready to pupate.

Besides spiders and caterpillars, the solitary wasps as a whole use a considerable variety of prey. Many choose flies, and others choose weevils. One species even drags frog-hopper nymphs from their cuckoo-spit hideouts. But whatever the kind of prey, each species of wasp usually confines itself to one species of prey. In a few species the sting venom actually kills rather than just paralyses the prey, but the dead food does not decay in the nest because the venom, circulated around the body of the prey at the time of the stinging, acts as an antiseptic, and prevents decay bacteria from developing.

Scorpions

Besides ants, wasps and bees, the only other animals to possess a sting are the scorpions. The abdomen of a scorpion is long and flexible, and it ends in a single

A scorpion attacking a lizard. The most dangerous scorpions are found in South and Central America, and also in North Africa.

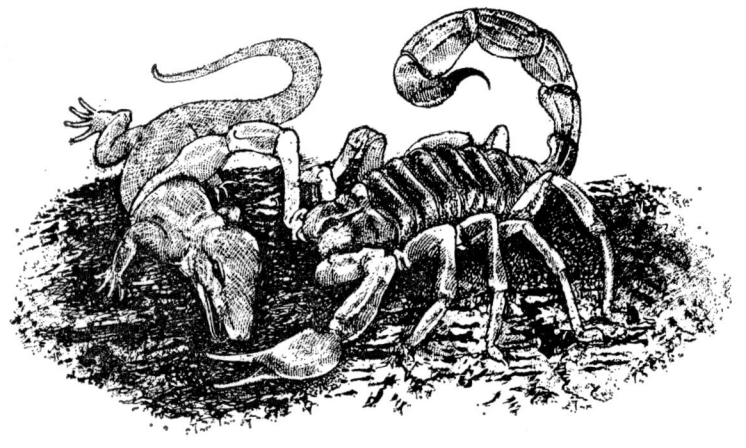

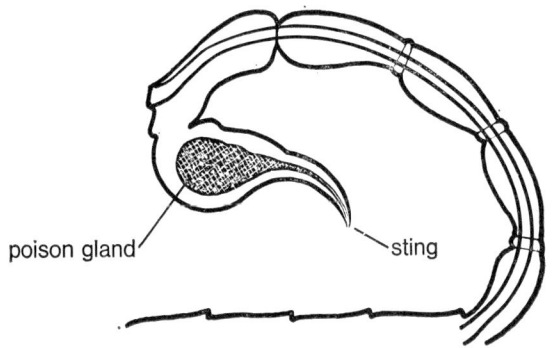

A diagram of the scorpion sting, situated at the end of the abdomen.

curved and sharply pointed sting which contains two venom glands opening near its tip.

Wherever scorpions occur they are feared by man, and not without reason, for the sting of the majority of them is dangerous. In the most dangerous kinds the venom is as toxic as that of the cobra, and a sting can kill a man in about four hours. Scorpions live in tropical and subtropical regions, and in those areas where the more dangerous types are common, antivenom sera are produced by methods similar to those used to produce sera for use against snake bite.

6
Chemical Warfare

All the animals we have considered so far not only produce poisonous substances, but have some means of injecting them into other animals. But there are a considerable number of animals, belonging to several different groups, which produce unpleasant chemical substances without being able to inject them. Most of these substances are not strictly poisonous, in that they cannot produce death, but they do have unpleasant consequences which help to deter their enemies from attacking them. They are thus defensive, rather than aggressive, and are seldom used to capture prey. In certain circumstances, though, some of them can be poisonous.

Man of course uses chemical warfare very extensively against insects. Though chemical insecticides fall outside the scope of this book, there is one kind of chemical warfare against insect pests which we must examine, as the chemicals used are produced by the victims themselves. Many male insects find their mates by an acute sense of smell which detects special courtship odours produced and dispersed in the air by females when they are ready for mating. These courtship attractants were first discovered by the great

CHEMICAL WARFARE

French naturalist J. H. Fabre in the nineteenth century. He was able to show that a female moth newly emerged from its chrysalis is able to attract males to her side from distances of up to several kilometres. Insects 'smell' with their antennae, and those of male moths are very large and feathery. In some insects it is the male which produces a courtship odour and the females which fly to him.

A great deal of investigation into insect attractants has been carried out in recent times, and we now know that each species and each sex has its own attractant substance, which is not produced by any other species or sex. This discovery gave rise to the suggestion that, if the chemist could analyse the attractant substances produced by insect pests and then devise a means of producing them in large quantities in the laboratory, it might be possible to use them to lure and trap the pests.

Two teams of scientists, one in Germany and one in America, worked on this project, and it took them twenty years before, in 1959, they both managed to produce an attractant artificially and in quantity. The German team worked on the silkworm moth. In order to obtain sufficient of the natural attractant for their chemical investigations, they had to squeeze out the minute contents from the abdominal scent glands of about half a million moths!

The American team worked on the gypsy moth, a serious pest of fruit and forest trees. It had been accidentally introduced from Europe in the 1890s. By 1959 it had not spread beyond New England, but here the

The male (left) and female gypsy moth, introduced accidentally into the United States from Europe.

caterpillars were causing extensive damage. The first critical trial of the new method of insect extermination took place in 1960. Fifty thousand moth traps were baited and distributed throughout all areas in New England where the gypsy moth was known to exist. The bait used in these traps had to be carefully mixed. It had three ingredients: the attractant which would lure the insects into the trap, some desirable material which the insects would eat, and a third poisonous ingredient which they would of course also swallow. This had to be tasteless to them or they might not eat the bait. This first experiment was a great success. Not only was the gypsy moth eliminated in New England, it was also prevented from spreading to any of the neighbouring states. It does not matter that in most cases only one sex is attracted and destroyed, because the members of the other sex cannot produce offspring without mates.

Following this initial success the American team then set about synthesizing the attractant of the Mediterranean fruit fly, which was causing severe devastation among the fruit orchards of Florida. Like the gypsy moth it had also been introduced accidentally from Europe. Once the attractant had been analysed and synthesized, it took but two years to rid the whole of Florida of the pest.

Another fruit fly, the Oriental fruit fly, was threatening to wipe out all the fruit trees on the Pacific island of Rota, one of the Mariana group of islands. Again the American team were successful in synthesizing the appropriate attractant. One thing both teams of research workers discovered was that not only were these attractants fairly simple chemical substances, they were all related to one another chemically. These two facts have made it easier than it might have been to synthesize other attractants.

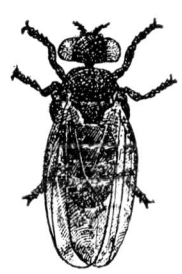

The notorious Mediterranean fruit fly, which caused havoc in European and American orchards before scientists began to work on insect attractants.

It is obvious that in the future attractants are going to play an increasing role in man's battle against insect pests. They have one great advantage over conventional insecticides. These often cause great damage to birds and other harmless animals which feed on the sprayed insects, whereas attractants affect only the chosen victims.

The chemists at an American pest control firm in Texas are now working on a similar method aimed at controlling and eliminating the common house fly.

POISON IN ANIMALS

They are making progress, but they have discovered that the amount of the attractant added to the bait must be carefully regulated. If too much is present the flies, after the first bite, which is not enough to kill them, seem to go quite mad, flying around at great speed and showing no further interest in the bait.

Fish

The production of warning substances by certain fish and other animals was first discovered by Professor Karl von Frisch about forty years ago. He happened to be watching a shoal of minnow fry swimming around in a pond, apparently quite contentedly, when a full-grown minnow appeared among them. They took no notice, because minnows are not afraid of one another. But the large minnow was apparently hungry and, as large minnows are likely to do if no other food is immediately available, it suddenly snapped at and ate one of the baby minnows. The remainder of the fry took no notice at all of what had happened. They made no attempt to flee the obvious danger. What did happen, though, was quite remarkable. As soon as the large minnow had bitten into the flesh of the baby minnow, it behaved as though in a panic, rushing away from the shoal of fry.

This seemed incredible behaviour. After all, it was the baby fish which should have swum off in panic. Further investigation revealed what had really happened. The skins of many kinds of fish possess glands

CHEMICAL WARFARE

which contain a certain shock substance. As soon as some of these glands are damaged, as in this case by the teeth of the large minnow, some of the shock substance is released into the water. This reacts on other adult fish in the same area, giving them a danger warning signal and causing them to swim away from the area as fast as possible. The baby fish did not flee because until they grow up they are insensitive to the warning substance.

The real purpose of these shock or warning substances is to cause other members of a species to flee when one of their number is attacked by a predator of another species. A subsequent experiment showed conclusively that the shock or warning substance was released when the skin of a fish was damaged. A single minnow from a shoal swimming in a pond was netted. Its skin was slightly grazed, and it was then put into a jar of water from the pond. After a few minutes the injured fish was removed from the jar and the water poured back into the pond among the shoal. The effect was immediate. The fish at once became agitated, exaggerating their breathing movements, before making off at full speed in all directions.

Further research has revealed an interesting fact. Only fish belonging to a single order, known to scientists as the Ostariophysis, produce these skin warning substances. The group includes all carp, salmon and catfish, and indeed two thirds of all freshwater fish. Other fish, such as sticklebacks, pike, trout and eels, which could well benefit from such a warning system, do not possess it. Nor do most sea fish. How many other animals possess the ability to produce warning substances we do not know, but certainly some species of snails and tadpoles do so.

Squids and cuttlefish

Squids and cuttlefish are close relatives of the octopus, and resemble it in many ways. They have powerful parrot-like beaks, and arms furnished with suckers, though they have ten of these instead of eight, two of them being much longer than the others.

Squids and cuttles lead a much more active life than the octopuses swimming in the open seas and seldom coming into inshore waters. In consequence their bodies are more streamlined, with a pair of flat, stabilizing fins along the sides. In the oceans there are some giant species with a total body and arm length exceeding seventeen metres. All squids and cuttles are predatory creatures, feeding mainly on fish. The smaller kinds show a preference for herring and mackerel, and since these are both fast swimmers, the

A cross-section of the squid showing the small sac which holds the inky liquid.

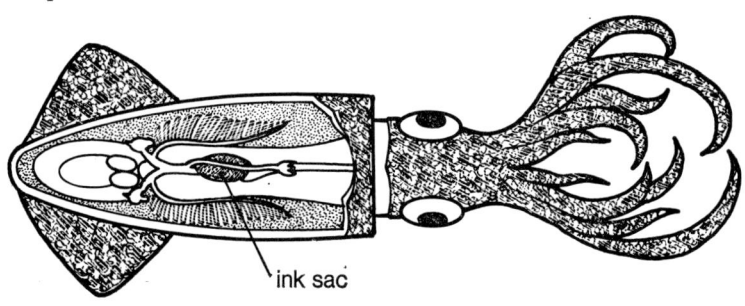

squids and cuttles must also be able to move swiftly to catch them. Movement is achieved by jet propulsion, a current of water being expelled under pressure through the respiratory tube or siphon. Since the opening of the siphon is at the front end of the body, the water jet drives the animal backwards. As it moves, it is able to make rapid changes of direction by using its stabilizing fins.

Speed alone, however, is not sufficient to enable squids and cuttles to escape from cod and other, larger fish which feed on them. But they do have a means of chemical defence. Alongside the siphon, and connected with it by a duct which is normally closed, is a bag known as the ink sac, which is filled with a dark-brown liquid. When pursued, the animal is able to squeeze the ink sac so that the inky fluid passes out with the water jet to form a dense cloud similar to the smoke screen laid down by ships in wartime. But squid and cuttle ink is more than just a smoke screen. Many fish have an acute sense of smell, and hunt more by scent than by sight. A straight smoke screen would be of little value, because the scent-hunter would still be able to follow its victim. The ink, however, contains a chemical substance that temporarily numbs the fish's sense of smell, and it loses contact.

Millipedes

Millipedes are entirely vegetarian, with weak jaws able to deal only with soft and often decaying vegetation.

A millipede. Despite its name, most millipedes have fewer than 200 legs. Whole groups of legs alternately contract and then move out so that the animal appears to be gliding over the ground.

Yet they are not defenceless. A considerable number of the body segments contain a pair of glands which open on the sides of the body. These produce an unpleasant liquid whose effects differ somewhat, depending upon the species.

The majority of millipedes, when they are handled, curl up into a spiral, and the liquid from these glands exudes gently from the pores, the animal having no means of forcing it out. It has quite a strong smell rather like iodine, and it stains the skin as iodine does. Investigations have shown that the liquid does, in fact, contain iodine, together with minute amounts of quinine, which is very bitter, chlorine and hydrocyanic acid. Chlorine and hydrocyanic acid are extremely poisonous substances, but the amounts present are too small to harm a predator. The liquid certainly is an effective deterrent to most animals, which will not eat millipedes. Only toads and birds are not put off by it.

Natives in parts of Mexico grind up certain kinds of millipedes to make a poison for tipping their arrows. Probably the deadly ingredient is the hydrocyanic acid. A number of individuals of these kinds of millipedes collected together in a confined space do produce a definite almond-like smell, and this is the smell of hydrocyanic acid.

In a few species the liquid does not just seep out from the glands, but is forced out under pressure by the contraction of muscles surrounding the glands. One species from Haiti is able to send out a broadside of deterrent spray for a distance of half a metre or more on either side of the body. Some of the giant tropical species, which may grow to a length of twenty-five centimetres or more, produce deterrent fluid which has a strong burning action. Contact with human skin causes it to blacken and die; as the skin peels off it leaves an ulcer which may take some weeks to heal.

Wood ant

Most ants possess stings, but not Britain's largest ant, the wood ant. This is the species which builds enormous nests, a metre or more in length and height, especially in pine forests. There is good evidence for believing that some of the largest nests may have been in existence and continuously occupied for as long as a hundred years. They contain countless thousands of ants.

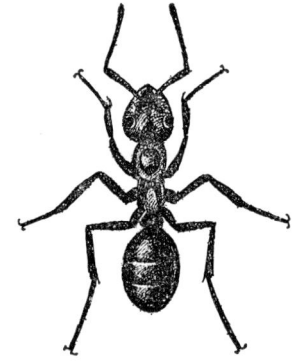

The wood ant. This ant kills prey but also feeds on honey dew.

Although the wood ant has no sting it is certainly not defenceless. At the tip of its abdomen are the openings of two glands, each filled with a milligram of formic acid, a volatile liquid with a pungent smell. If alarmed by the approach of an enemy, the ant raises its body as high as it can off the ground by standing on the tips of its legs, curves its abdomen forward beneath the rest of the body, and squirts a fine jet of acid at the enemy. Although its body is somewhat less than twelve millimetres long, the contraction of the muscles surrounding its acid glands is so powerful that the jet can be projected thirty centimetres or more. If a nest is disturbed, thousands of ants rush out to defend it, each discharging its glands, so that the pungent fumes of formic acid can be detected some considerable distance away from the nest. Wood ants also have acid glands in their head, connected to their powerful jaws. Any ant meeting an intruder, or any small animal suitable as food, will give it a very painful and often fatal bite, for its jaws will inject the acid into the wound.

CHEMICAL WARFARE

Bombardier beetle

The bombardier beetle is often chased by larger carnivorous beetles. As it runs away, it emits a small quantity of very volatile liquid in the face of its pursuer. This liquid evaporates instantly to form a tiny cloud of extremely unpleasant pungent vapour, distracting the pursuer just long enough to give the bombardier beetle a good chance of escaping. The name bombardier refers to the fact that as the glands are discharged they produce a peculiar explosive sound like a rifle shot. The snag with glands which discharge their contents is that it takes some time for them to be recharged after they have been used, and during this time of course the insect remains defenceless.

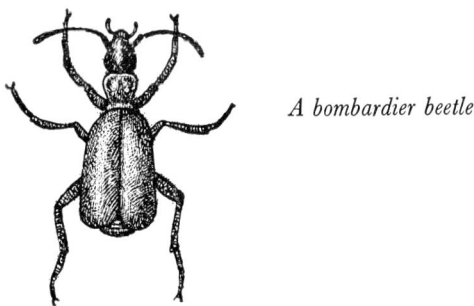

A bombardier beetle.

Puss moth caterpillar

The caterpillar of the puss moth has a gland producing formic acid beneath its mouth, which it employs for a

POISON IN ANIMALS

particular purpose. Certain ichneumon flies lay their eggs on puss moth caterpillars, and whenever the caterpillar sees one approaching it discharges a jet of formic acid towards it. If it succeeds in hitting its target the fly will retreat. If not, then the fly can go ahead and lay its eggs, because the acid gland will now be useless until it has had time to recharge. The tiny larvae which hatch from these eggs begin eating the body of the caterpillar from inside, eventually killing it.

Spanish fly

Despite its name the Spanish fly is really a small beetle. The liquid it produces as soon as it is touched causes intense irritation resulting in skin blisters. The active chemical substance contained in the secretion is known as cantharidin, which was once used in medi-

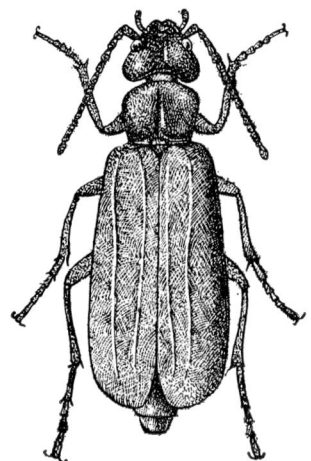

A Spanish fly.

CHEMICAL WARFARE

cine. It is still used today, mixed with bay rum, to produce hair restorers. Whether these work seems doubtful!

Frogs and toads

Many frogs and toads rely upon poisonous and distasteful skin secretions for protection. In many toads the glands producing these secretions are collected together in groups which are responsible for their warty appearance. Most animals seem to know the unpleasant consequences of seizing frogs or toads in their mouths and leave them severely alone. If a dog should pick one up, it will soon drop it and shake its head in obvious discomfort.

A marine toad.

poison gland

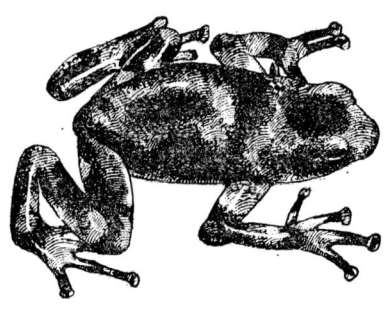

Dendrobates – *a South American tree frog. Its skin secretions are used by native Indians as poison for their arrow-tips. The secretions of another South American tree frog,* Phyllobates, *is said to contain one of the strongest poisons known.*

Experiments have shown that the poison contained in these secretions acts upon the heart and the nervous system, death resulting from stoppage of the heart. Injection of a small quantity of the skin secretion of the edible frog into a small bird caused death within a minute, and the edible frog is not one of the more poisonous species. In South America there is a group of frogs whose skin secretions really are deadly, and these have been used by the natives from very early times to tip their poison arrows. The tiniest drop introduced into a wound is sufficient to kill a man.

Sea cucumber

The sea cucumber, a relative of the starfishes and the sea-urchins, has no special poison glands but has poison distributed in its tissues. Sea cucumbers really do look something like rather short cucumbers as they lie on their sides, more or less motionless, on the sea bed or at the bottom of a rock pool. Whether or not this

CHEMICAL WARFARE

poison serves any useful purpose so far as the sea cucumber is concerned, we do not know. It certainly has no means of passing the poison out of its body through special glands in order to defend itself against a predator which attacks it. On the other hand, there is evidence that the poison does get into the water, presumably passing out slowly through the general surface of the skin. Fish and other marine animals put into an aquarium tank in which sea cucumbers have previously been living usually die. So perhaps the poison does serve to give a general warning to other animals to keep clear.

The natives of many Pacific Islands have known for a very long time that sea cucumbers are poisonous. A traditional method of catching fish is to drop the cut-up bodies of sea cucumbers into coral reef pools. In a short time this brings any fish in the pool to the surface, where they can be very easily caught because they are semi-paralysed.

Despite being poisonous to many animals, sea cucumbers seem to be harmless to man. They are eaten in many parts of the world. Usually they are cooked,

The sea cucumber uses its tentacles to push mud and sand into its mouth. Organic matter in the mud is then digested as food. Despite its unattractive appearance, a certain kind of sea cucumber – trepang – is eaten by man.

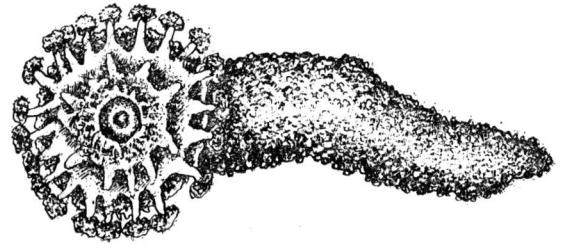

POISON IN ANIMALS

either fresh or after having been dried, and this may possibly destroy the poison, but at least two species, known to be poisonous to fish, are eaten raw in Japan without any ill effects.

A skunk turns its back on a racoon and discharges its foul-smelling fluid. The skunk, which is about the size of a small cat, is restricted to America.

CHEMICAL WARFARE

Skunk

Scent glands play an important part in the lives of all carnivorous mammals. They are situated beneath the base of the tail, and produce exceedingly strong-smelling liquids, which are often so repulsive to our

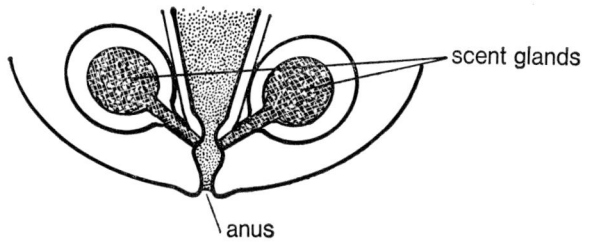

The skunk's scent glands are situated at the base of the tail, near the anus.

sense of smell that it might be better to call them stink glands. Most carnivores tend to be solitary creatures, and at the breeding season the scent trails which they lay enable the sexes to find each other. Scent is also used for marking out territory, and this serves to warn off other members of the same species.

One of the smaller carnivores, the skunk, has extended the use of its scent glands to include protection against other animals. The scent of the skunk is probably worse than any other smell produced in nature, and it certainly knows how to use it. If any animal, however large, so much as moves in the direction of a skunk without any aggressive intent – often without even knowing there is a skunk around – the skunk will not move out of the way as most other animals would. Instead it turns its back on the approaching intruder and squirts a jet of the evil-smelling liquid towards it, and this is sufficient to cause it to make a rapid retreat. Often the victim will be violently sick. Although the scent is not poisonous, its use certainly does represent highly efficient chemical warfare.

CHEMICAL WARFARE

Any clothing contaminated with the smallest drop must be destroyed, for it is impossible to get rid of the smell. The smell of a discharge can travel considerable distances. Charles Darwin's South American guide told him that a skunk can sometimes be detected five kilometres away. And Darwin himself wrote that 'more than once, when entering the harbour at Monte Video, the wind being offshore, we have perceived the odour on board the *Beagle*'.

Index
of Animals

Adder, death, 32
  European, 36, 38
  puff, 36, 37
Ants, 67
  wood, 85–6
Asthenosoma varium, 48
Atrax robustus, 22
Aurelia, 59

Bees, 64–7
Beetle, bombardier, 87
Blarina brevicauda, 10
Boomslang, 32
Bushmaster, 38

Caterpillars, 39–40, 51–3, 87–8
Cobra, 26, 30–31, 32
  black-necked, 34
  king, 25, 32
  ringhals, 34
Colubridae, 31
Conus geographus, 18
Copperhead, 38
Cuttlefish, 82–3

Dendrobates, 90
Diadema, 46–8

Eel, moray, 12–13
Elapidae, 32

Fer-de-lance, 38
Fish, 40–46
  dragon, 43–5
  stone, 44, 45–6
  weever, 40–42
Fly, house, 79–80
  Mediterranean fruit, 78–9
  Oriental fruit, 79
  Spanish, 88–9
Frogs, 89–90

Hamadryad, 32

Jellyfish, 54, 59–60

Krait, 32

Mamba, 32
Millipedes, 83–5
Minnow, 80–81
Moccasin, 38
Mole, 11–12
Moth, brown-tail, 52–3
  gypsy, 77–8
  puss, 87–8
  silkworm, 77
  yellow-tail, 51

Octopus, ringed, 14–15

Phyllobates, 90
Portuguese man-of-war, 60–2
Pycnopodia, 50, 51

Rattlesnake, 25–6, 38

Scorpions, 74–5
Sea anemones, 54–9
Sea cucumber, 90–92
Sea-urchins, 39, 46–51
Sea wasp, 8, 60
Shrew, 9–11
Skunk, 92, 93–5
Snails, 16–18
Snakes, 24–37
  coral, 32
  sea, 35–6
  tiger, 32
Spiders, 19–23, 69
Squids, 82–3
Starfish, 48, 50, 51
Sting ray, 42–3

Tarantula, 20–22
Toads, 89–90
Toxopneustes, 49–51

Vipers, 36–8
  gaboon, 36, 37
  pit, 38
  Russell's, 36, 37

Wasps, 68–74
  common, 68
  mason (potter), 72–3
  sand, 71–2
  spider, 69–71